ARTIST ARCHIVES™ INTRODUCTION BY MAX ALLAN COLLINS

SWIMSUIT SWEETIES

PORTLAND, OREGON

SWIMSUIT SWEETIES

INTRODUCTION

Design Principia Graphica
Technical Assistance Hoover H.Y. Li
Editor Ann Granning Bennett

The publisher would like to extend a special thanks to LeRoy Darwin for supplying various images in this book.

Printed in China

Library of Congress Cataloging-in-Publication Data
Collins, Max Allan.
Swimsuit sweeties / Max Allan Collins. — 1st American ed.
p. cm. — (Artist archives)
ISBN 1-888054-35-2 (pbk. : alk. paper)
1. Feminine beauty (Aesthetics) — United States. 2. Pinup art — United States. I. Title. II. Series.
N7630.C75 1999
769'.424— dc21 99-28110
CIP

9 8 7 6 5 4 3 2

FOR A FREE CATALOG WRITE TO COLLECTORS PRESS, INC.

P.O. Box 230986
Portland, Oregon 97281
Toll Free 800-423-1848
Or visit our website at *www.collectorspress.com*

THE SWIMSUIT — or at least what swimwear evolved into, by the mid-1930s — was a license to thrill for the men and women who fashioned the calendar beauties, the pin-up queens, who would enliven the walls of fraternal lodges, car-repair shops, barbershops, and barracks throughout the mid-twentieth century. Without the colorful second skin of the socially acceptable swimsuit, key artists such as George Petty, Alberto Vargas, and Gil Elvgren could not have gotten away with exposing the flesh and forms of their fantasy females.

Petty, Vargas, and Elvgren were only three of dozens of purveyors of pulchritude working in calendar and pin-up art from the 1930s through the early 1960s. Many other gifted commercial artists recorded and shaped the standard of American female beauty throughout those years — among them, Billy DeVorss, Jules Erbit, Zoë Mozert, Roy Best, Bill Medcalf, and Art Frahm. These and other artists, and their beautiful creations, will take center stage in these pages.

But first the swimsuit — because, without it, where would these beautiful women be? We'll pause to reflect on that for a moment and move to a brief history lesson.

In the late 1800s in America, bathing suits were chaste celebrations of wool serge, with full sleeves, knee-length skirts, ankle-length pantalets, shoes, stockings, and, of course, a tied-under-the-chin bonnet. Two people changed all that, popular culture forces to be reckoned with: Australian swimming star Ahnette Kellerman and filmmaker Mack Sennett.

Champion exhibition swimmer Kellerman had taken up swimming after a childhood bout with polio. In diving and marathon races, she competed against men in the Thames and Seine rivers and toured America in a shocking one-piece diving suit. This body stocking (in some instances, flesh-colored) came as close to public nudity as any prominent woman had dared, probably since Lady Godiva. She was arrested at a public beach, which of course only made her a bigger celebrity, even a movie star.

And speaking of movies, Mack Sennett's early twentieth-century bathing beauties — sporting the briefer, form-fitting attire Kellerman had inspired in swimwear designers and manufacturers — enlivened silent comedies and posed for countless publicity stills, paving the way for decades of swimsuit posing in publicity shots by starlets and stars alike.

The efforts of Kellerman and Sennett were encouraged by the health and fitness fad that followed World War One. Nobel Prize-winner Marie Curie was a vocal proponent of the health benefits of sea-bathing and open-air sports. She denounced frilly ankle-length bloomers and extolled the practicality of sleeker, simpler swimsuits.

As the 1920s moved toward the 1930s, women's swimwear took on the recognizable style that has endured for decades. Backless suits appeared in the early 1930s, and by late in that decade, geometric windows were occasionally cut out of the center front for a glimpse of flesh, foreshadowing the next decade's two-piece suit and the bikini to come.

The images in this book chart the innocent sensuality of an art form once thought racy, now considered (by all but politically correct prigs) nostalgic fun. Our *Swimsuit Sweeties* begin in the mid-1930s and extend to the start of the 1960s, by which time the photographic pin-ups of *Playboy* had trumped the lovely painted bathing beauties of artists like Billy DeVorss and Jules Erbit with airbrushed nude "reality."

Billy DeVorss was born in 1908 in St. Joseph, Missouri; his parents supported his artistic bent, and he developed his skills by imitating Rolf Armstrong and other top commercial talents. Working as a teller in a St. Joe bank, DeVorss found a perfect model in a lovely local girl named Glenna — and married her. DeVorss attended Kansas City Art Institute, graduating in 1934 but arrived at the school self-taught, his distinctive style in full bloom. He studied only to refine his drafting skills and learn color theory.

In Rolf Armstrong, DeVorss had chosen a role model whose approach, however skillful, was of another time. Fortunately, DeVorss proved more moldable to changing tastes than his hero, moving into the 1940s with considerable ease, able to let go of the bee-stung-lipped flapper that Armstrong dragged bodily into the Swing era. A DeVorss girl is of her time, beaming with unashamed sexuality, self-confident, poised, beautiful, and yet somehow wholesome.

The Armstrong influence is in full sway in "Water Proofed," from the floppy hat of the radiant brunette to her long limbs, as well as the regal, Joan Crawford-ish attitude she displays; the sleekness of the braless swimsuit, however, reveals an unexpected dash of George Petty.

"Pink Lady" finds DeVorss at his most charming, the pink of the swimsuit nicely startling against the solid black background, perked by abstract dashes of color as the voluptuous blonde leans against some unspecified surface. A contradiction in DeVorss' style is his peculiar ability to be awkward and graceful simultaneously — the model seems stiff and yet fluid, as if her confidence is in part a mask.

The 1946 "Pose Please" reveals DeVorss' ability to take the Armstrong style — the eyes and eyebrows and eyelashes could belong to a pin-up of a decade earlier — into a new era. The adorable blonde's lips carry a hint of the bee-stung Clara Bow look, but plumped into something more provocative, less coy, more confident — and the backdrop is just a solid color now, no abstract splash of Armstrong-esque color behind her, the golden glow of her hair boldly positioned against yellow. The skin-tight swimsuit with matching high heels makes for simple, perfect costuming of a sleekly rendered pin-up rivaling Vargas and Petty.

DeVorss was only one of many artists under Armstrong's spell — witness Victor Tchechet's "Sittin' Pretty," or consider famous female pin-up artist, Zoë Mozert (1907–1993), an exemplary disciple of Armstrong's pastel style. Often her own model, Mozert rejected sexy-girl clichés in favor of depicting young women with recognizably individual features and personalities. In her "Sunshine Beauty," Mozert uses the Armstrong floppy hat as a prop and positions her pretty subject against Armstrong blue; but the girl has a naturalness, the pose a casualness, all the artist's own.

Though Jules Erbit's expert use of pastels for his glowing beauties places him among Rolf Armstrong followers, the artist differs from DeVorss by exhibiting his own distinctive style. Budapest-born Erbit was one of America's most prolific pin-up artists from the early 1930s until he retired in 1950. His lovely women graced calendars, posters, and prints, and his advertising accounts included Palmolive Soap and other prominent clients; he retired from pin-ups and advertising to a successful career in portraiture.

Bathing-suit beauties are rare among the works of Erbit, who specialized in more sedate, quietly sensual images — a lovely woman in a gown lounging in a garden or leaning against an oceanliner railing. Erbit exemplifies the glamour approach — a soft-focus, flowers-in-the-hair world of prom queens, debutantes, and socialites.

But even a prom queen goes swimming now and then, as the radiant, windswept, caped strawberry blonde of Erbit's 1938 "Breezing Beauty" herein would indicate. A surprising hint of nipple gives a sensual reality to a slender figure whose white swimsuit pops boldly out of a solid blue background. Erbit's earlier 1936 "Ready for a Dip" is perched on a diving board against a fully rendered backdrop of cloud-dappled sky and sailboat-dotted sea, the red—swimsuited, long-limbed lass exuding wholesomeness.

His other diving-board beauty — "Tops 'Em All" — seems more sophisticated, and the solid black background emphasizes the sensual reality of her curvy, slender figure; though he did lengthen limbs at times, Erbit rendered beauties in a fashion that tends not to exhibit exaggerated male notions or pulchritude so common in the genre.

Considered one of Erbit's most famous works (pin-up authority Charles Martignette cites it as a million-copy seller calendar), "Swing Time" — also known as "All-American Swinger" — is a fine example of Erbit at his subtly sexiest. Cloaked in a pale yellow swimsuit, the redhead's slender yet full figure — again, the buds of her breasts are gently indicated — jumps out against a solid blue background in a strikingly simple diagonal design.

Ohio-born Roy Best was a versatile and successful illustrator whose credits include *Saturday Evening Post* covers and children's book illustrations for Whitman publishing, notably *The Peter Pan Picture Book*. Best was also one of Brown & Bigelow's top calendar-girl artists throughout the 1940s (Best had already done a number of art-deco nudes and pin-ups in the 1930s for other companies).

Trained at the famous School of the Art Institute of Chicago, Best was one of the few pastel masters not particularly under Armstrong's sway. His 1940s pin-ups are so modern that they might have been created a decade or two later, witness the sparkling, Marilyn Monroe-like "The Beach Queen"; the sunglasses-removing blonde is caught in a natural pose, and the subtle pinks, greens, and yellows of the piece create a simmer mood. Another lovely Best blonde — "The Mermaid" — strikes a more traditional pin-up pose, yet the artist conveys a naturalness that eludes many of his peers. Best's girls are less exaggerated than many pin-up queens, their figures lovely but credible, supple yet possible.

Bill Medcalf is one of the great unsung heroes of pin-up art. Of all the talented artists who followed Gil Elvgren's lead into oils, Medcalf — who idolized Elvgren — is the master's nearest equal, turning out lushly rendered oil paintings of gorgeous all-American girls, who display (in the artist's words) "sex appeal but without sophistication, like someone's sweet sister."

Minneapolis-born Medcalf would seem destined to work for Brown & Bigelow, and he did, handling special-project calendar commissions for top advertising accounts such as Sylvania ("Miss Sylvania") and Kelly Springfield Tires. His "Surf's Up" pictured in this volume depicts a sunny, curvaceous blonde on a surfboard, casting us an Elvgren-style pursed kiss.

Versatile Art Frahm — another Chicago artist trained at the Art Institute's school — compares favorably with such master technicians in oil as Elvgren and Medcalf. Oddly, his two most famous approaches were sharply contrasting: he specialized in depicting perfectly coifed, daringly décolletaged, ball-gown beauties, aglow in romantic soft-focus settings; but he also created the campy, sexist "embarrassment" series, in which a lovely young thing is literally caught with her lacy panties down to her ankles while she's bowling, walking the dog, or changing a tire.

Whether portraying moonlight romance or daylight chagrin, the successful Frahm — whose commercial clients included the likes of Coca-Cola, Quaker Oats, Libby Foods, and Schlitz Beer — created some very attractive pin-ups. "Yours For the Basking" displays an all-American beauty who is either doing up, or undoing, a bikini top that unabashedly outlines the contours of her breasts.

By the early 1960s, bathing beauties had franker times to compete with. In "Laughing Eyes" by "John Shilling" (a pseudonym for Chicago-born portrait artist Jack Whittrup), it's come off entirely. Fashions might change, but swimsuit sweeties likely will remain a permanent fixture of the American landscape — just ask 'em at *Sports Illustrated*.

Sources: *Sensual Swimwear*, Roger Blair, Crescent Books, 1991; *Bathing Beauties*, Michael Calmer, Sphere, 1977; *The Great American Pin-Up*, Charles S. Martignette and Louis K. Meisel, Taschen, 1996.

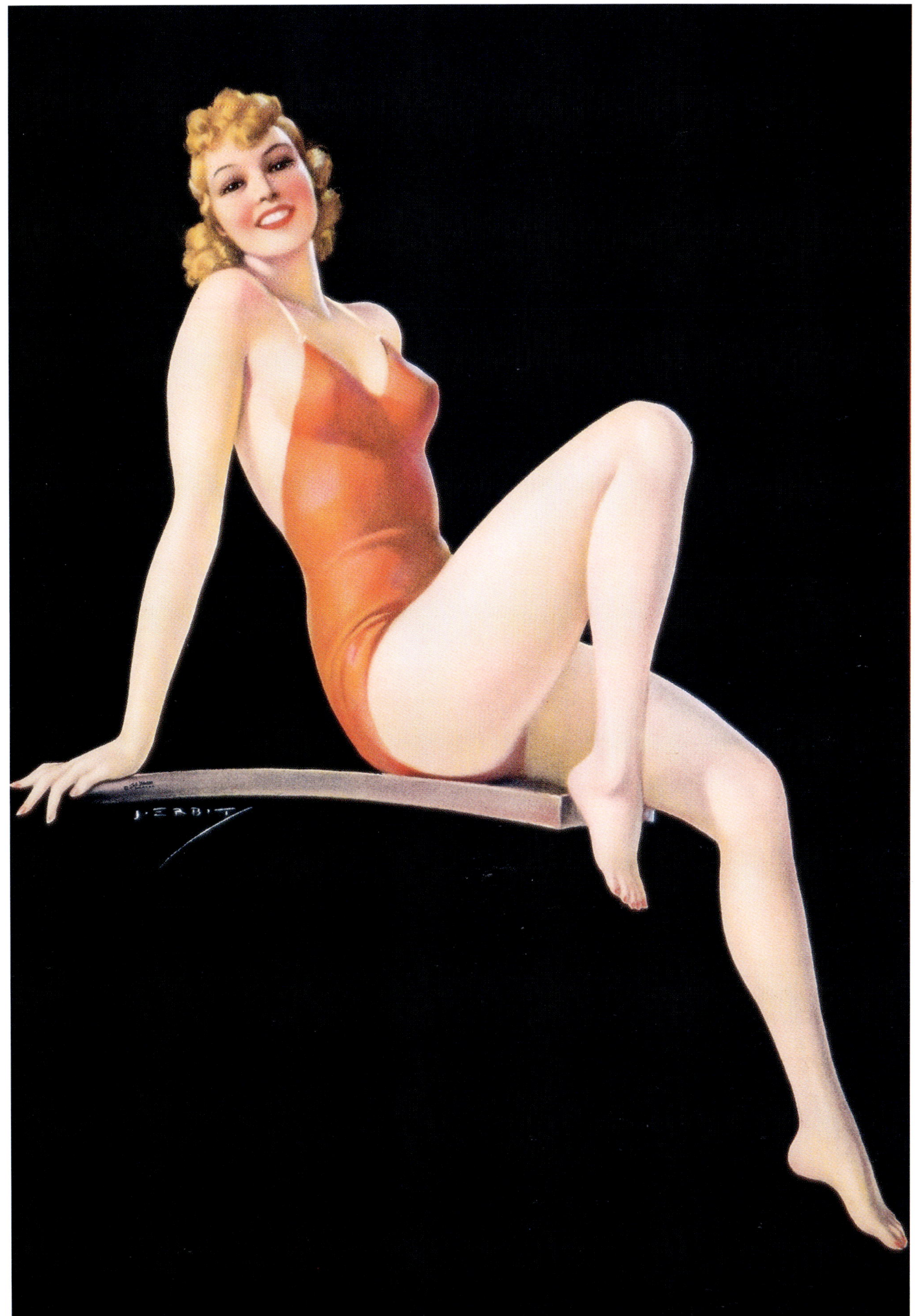
J. ERBIT

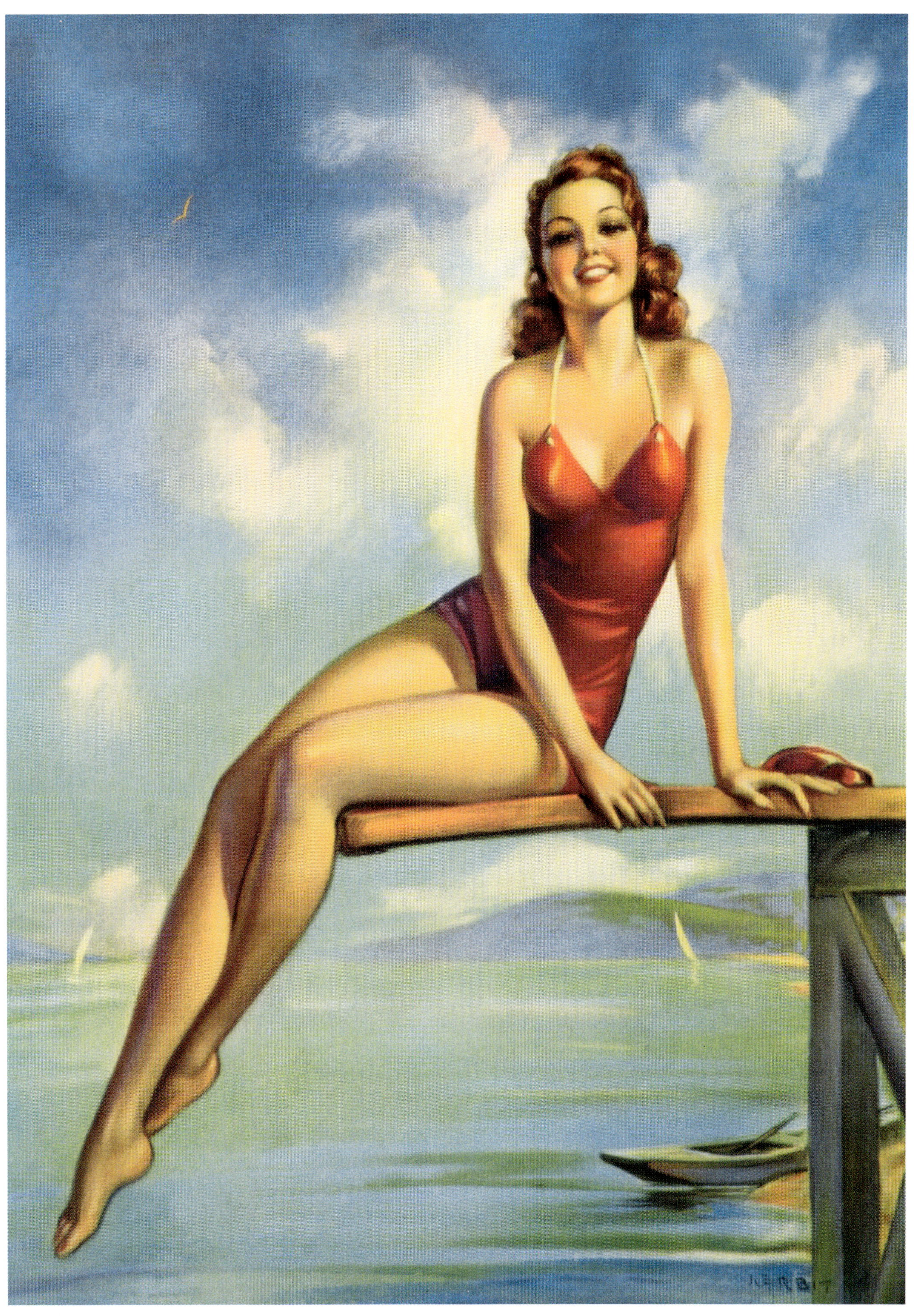

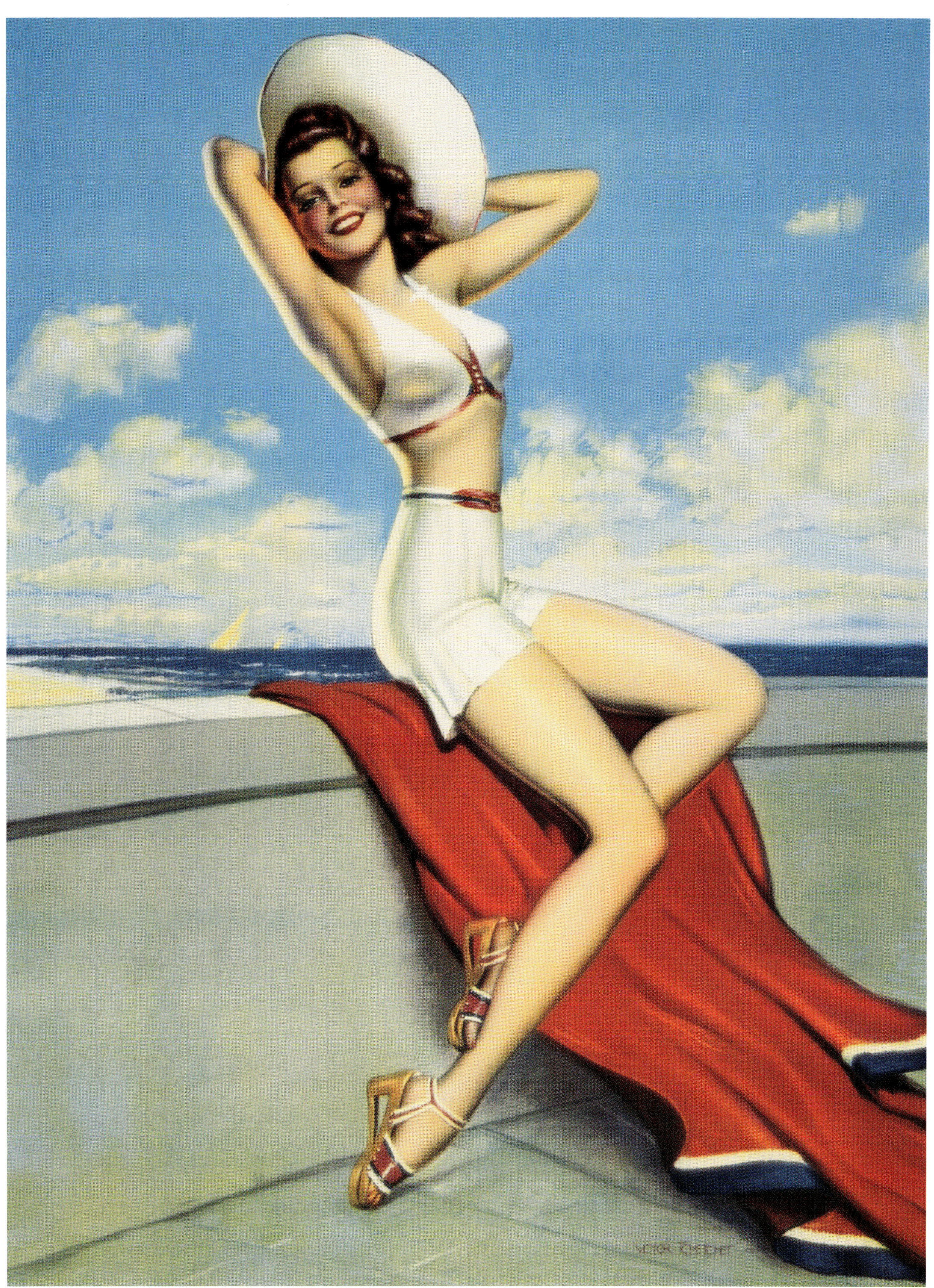

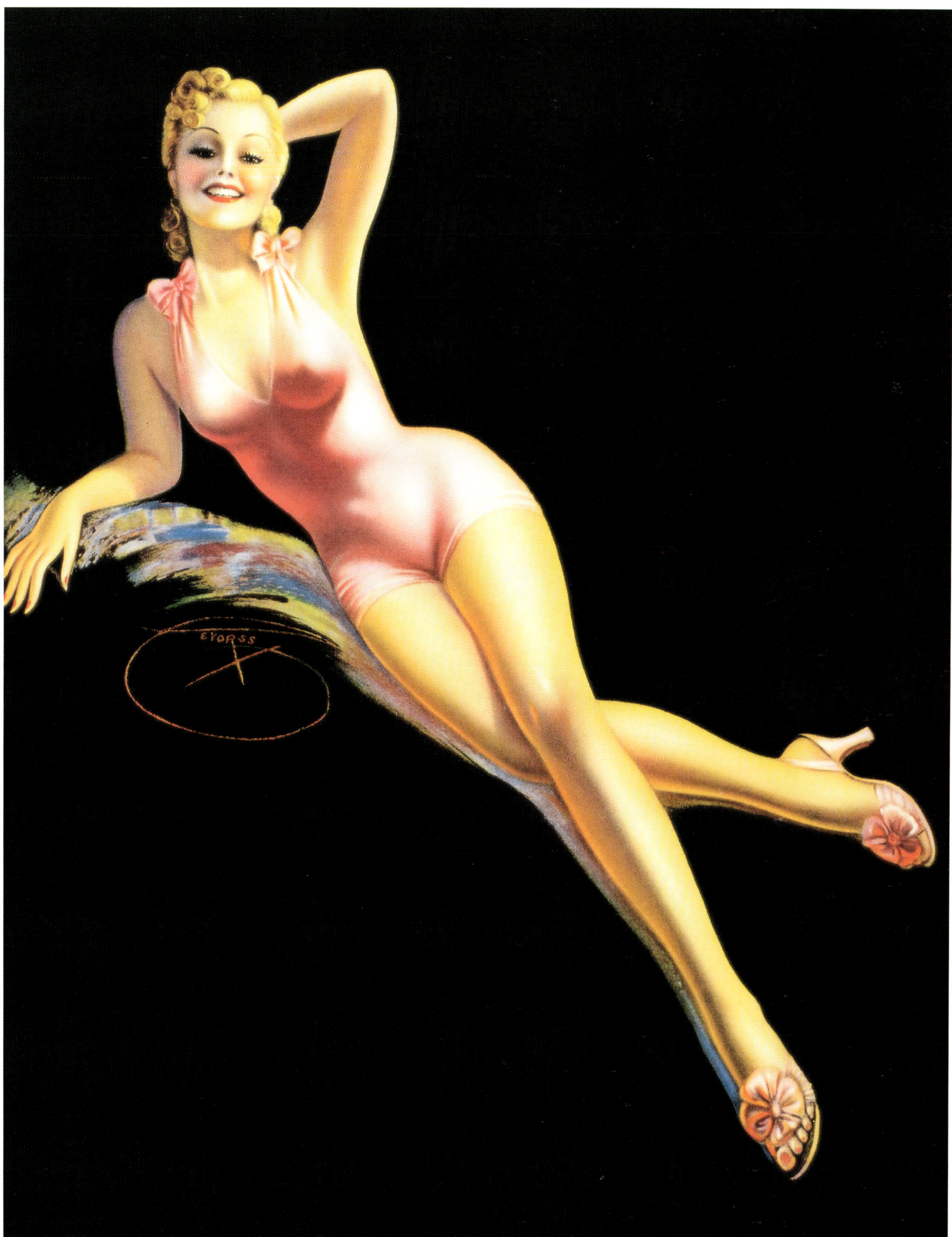
EVORSS

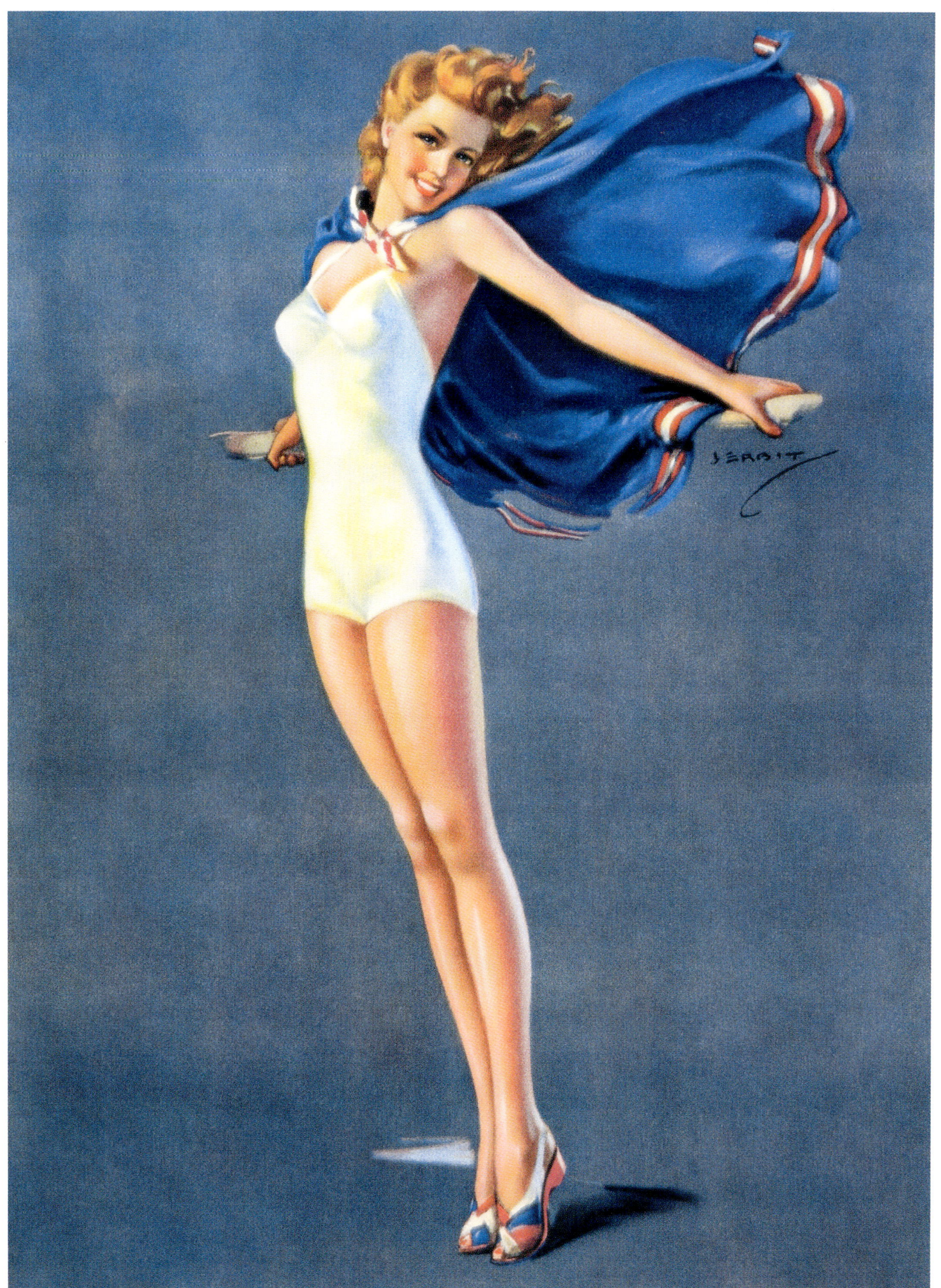

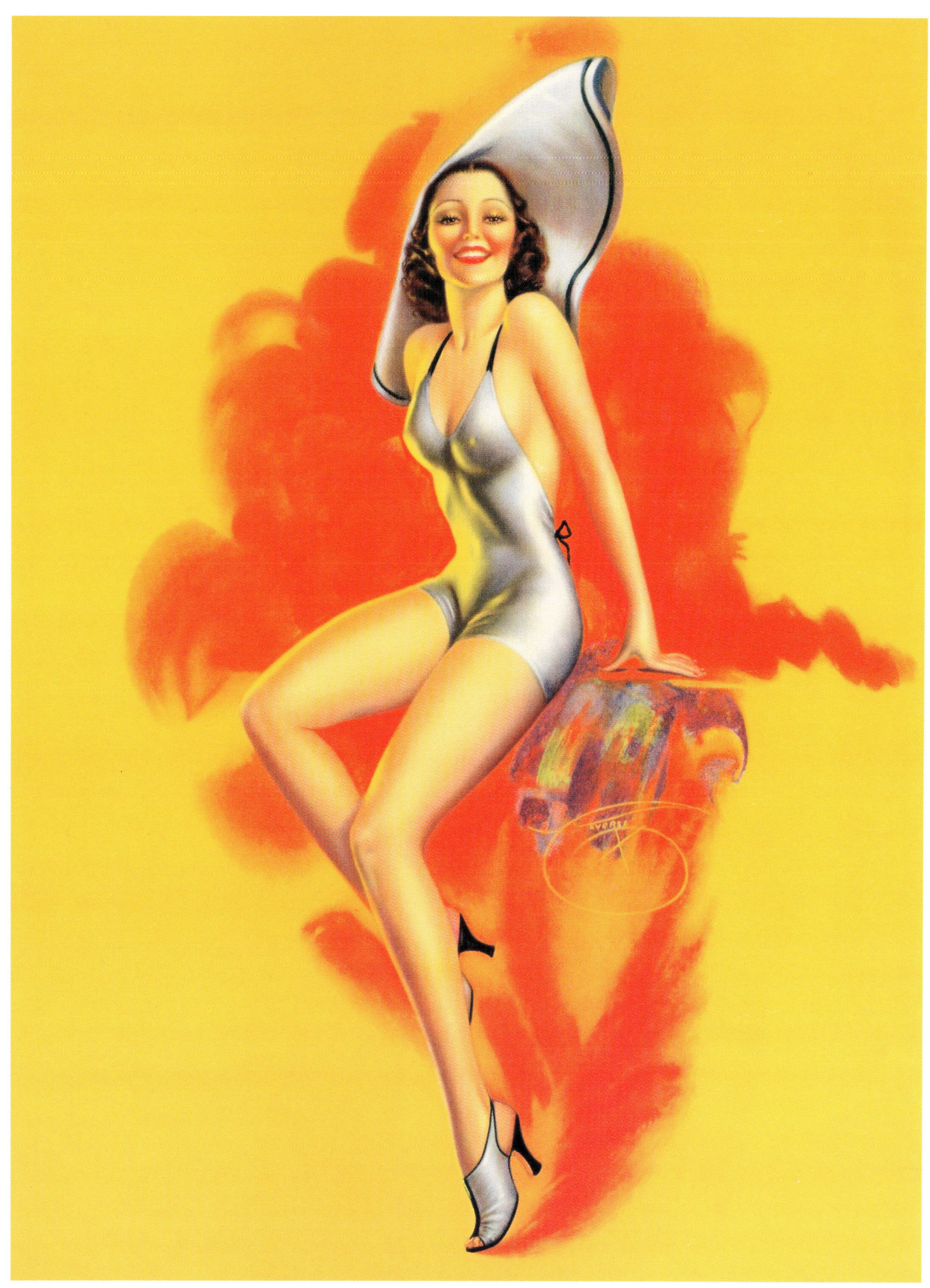

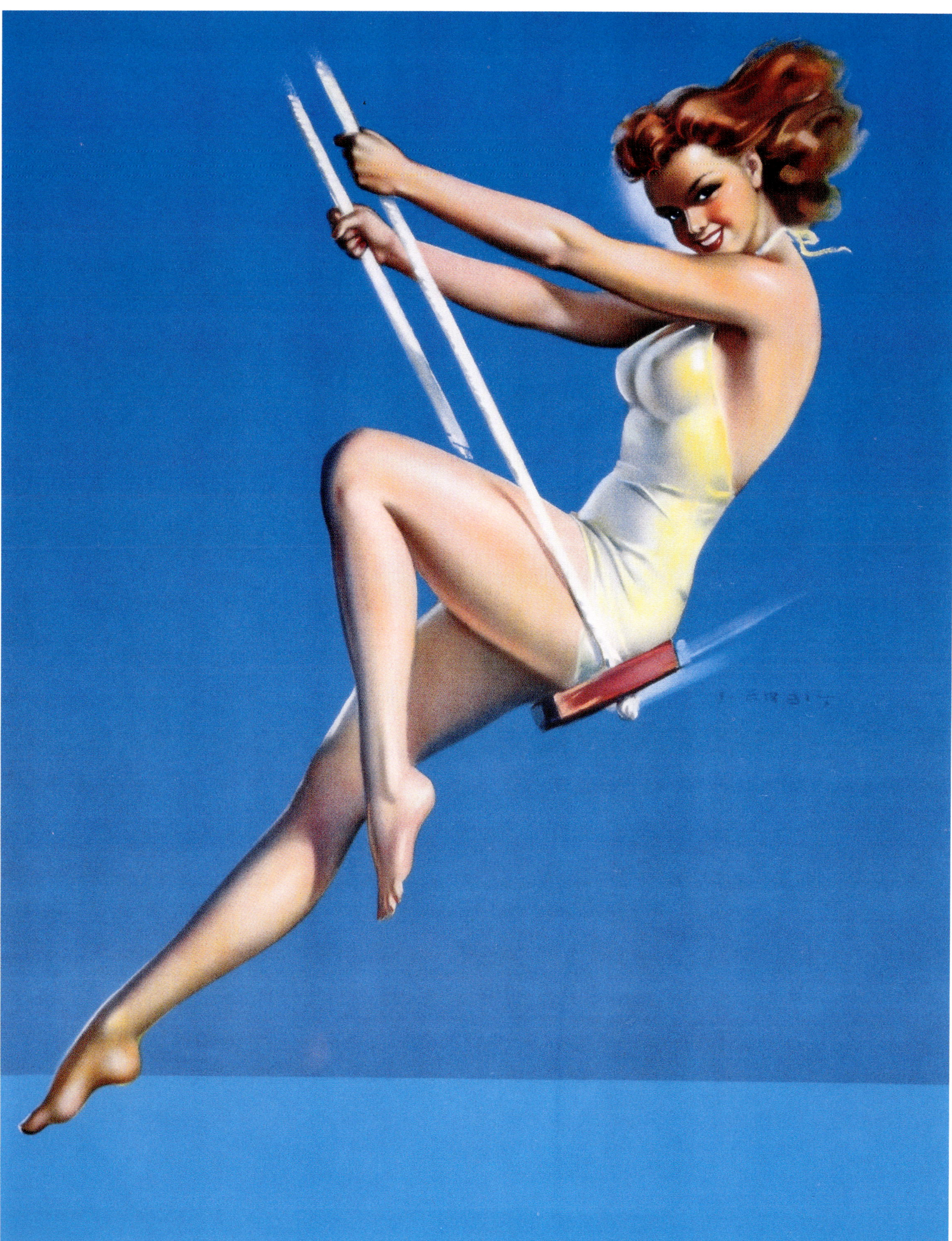

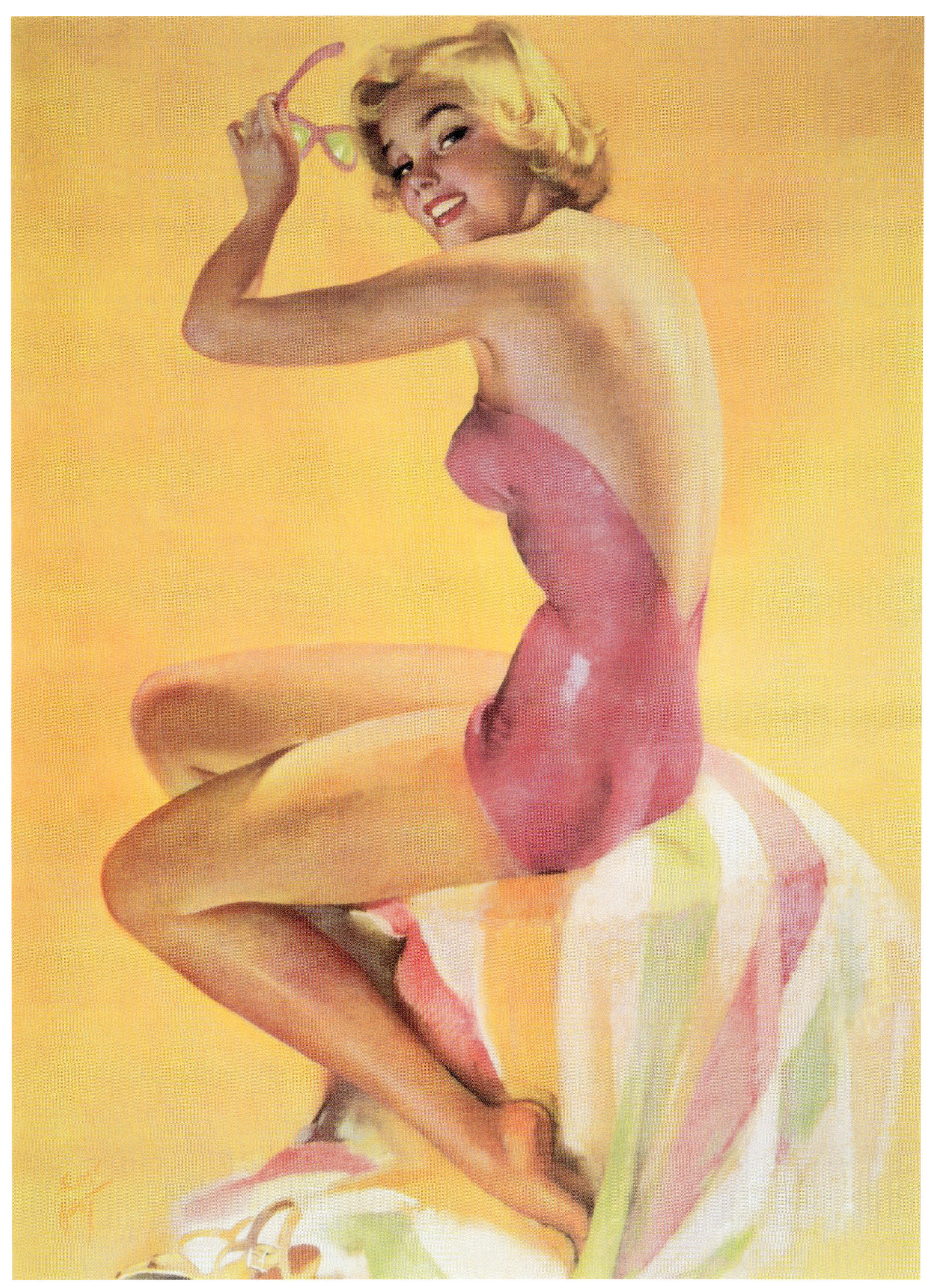

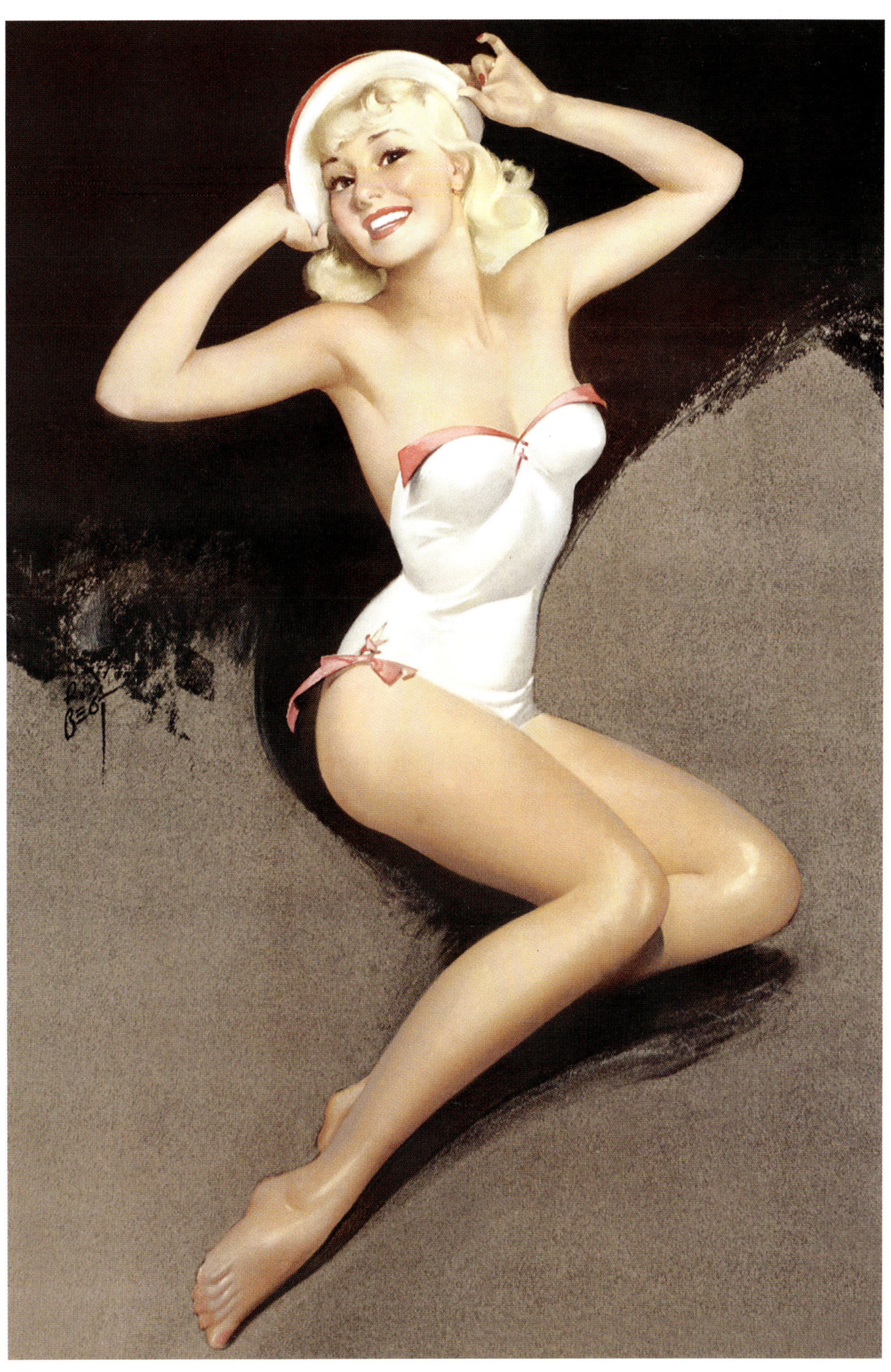

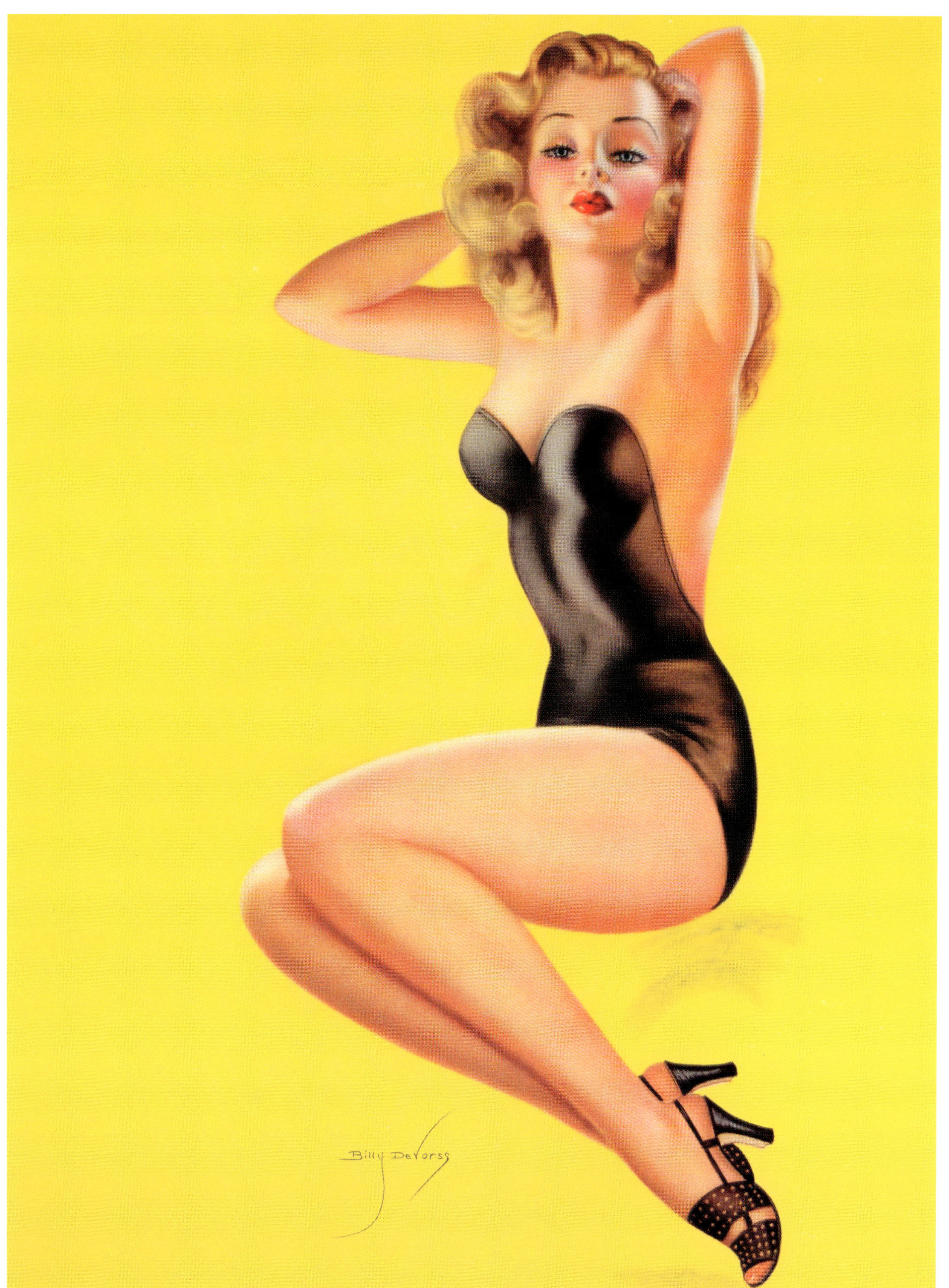
Billy DeVorss

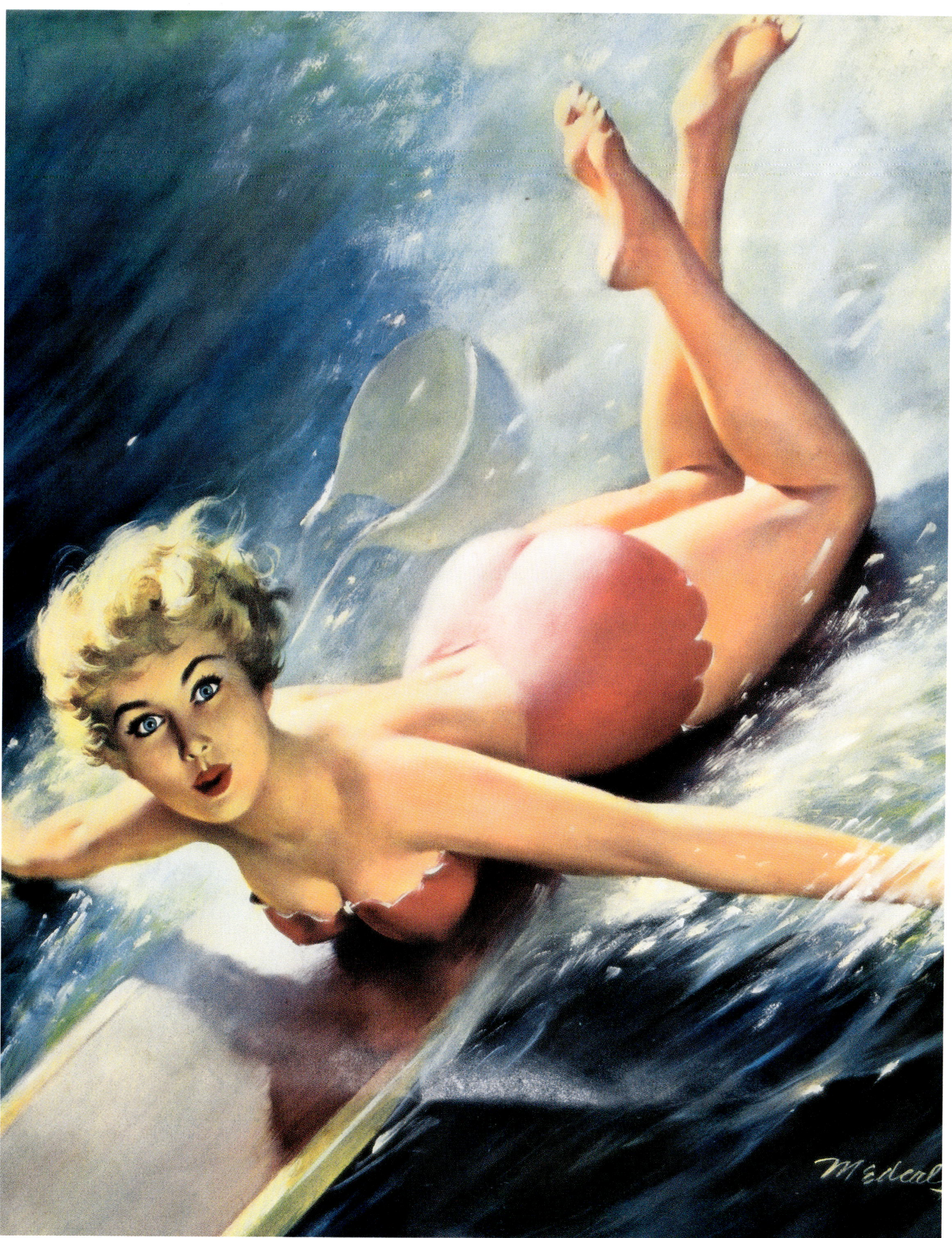

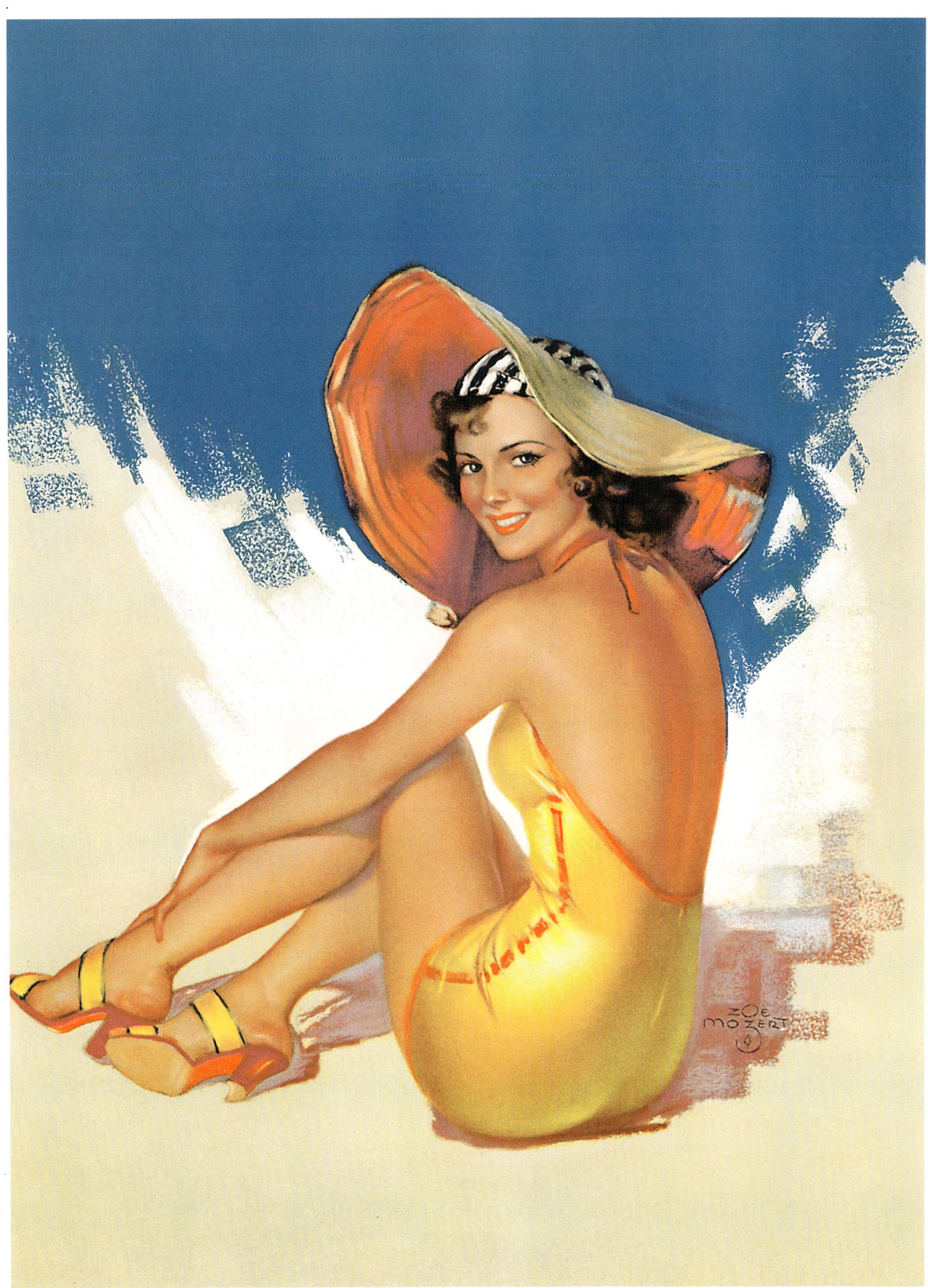
ZOE
MOZERT

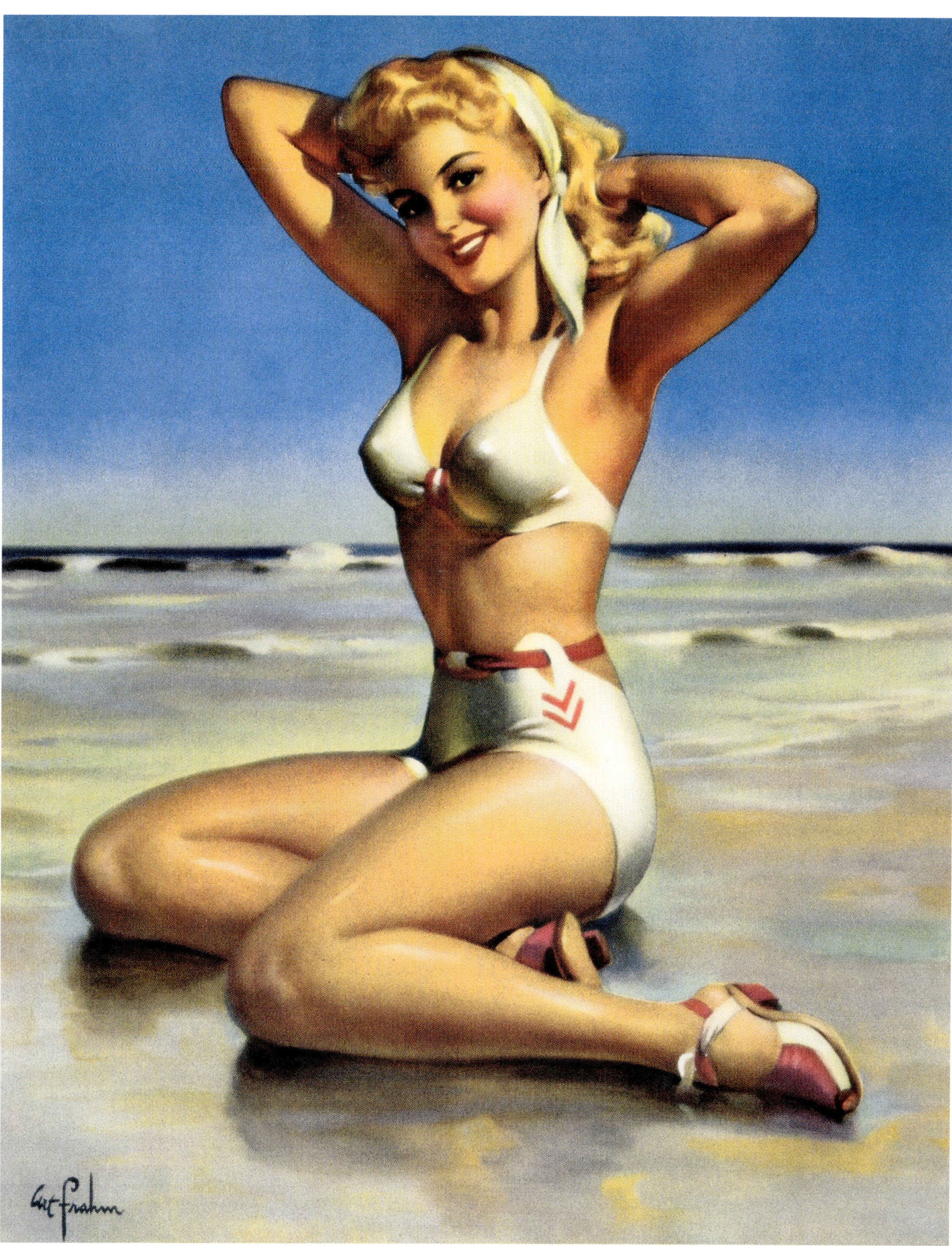
Art Frahm

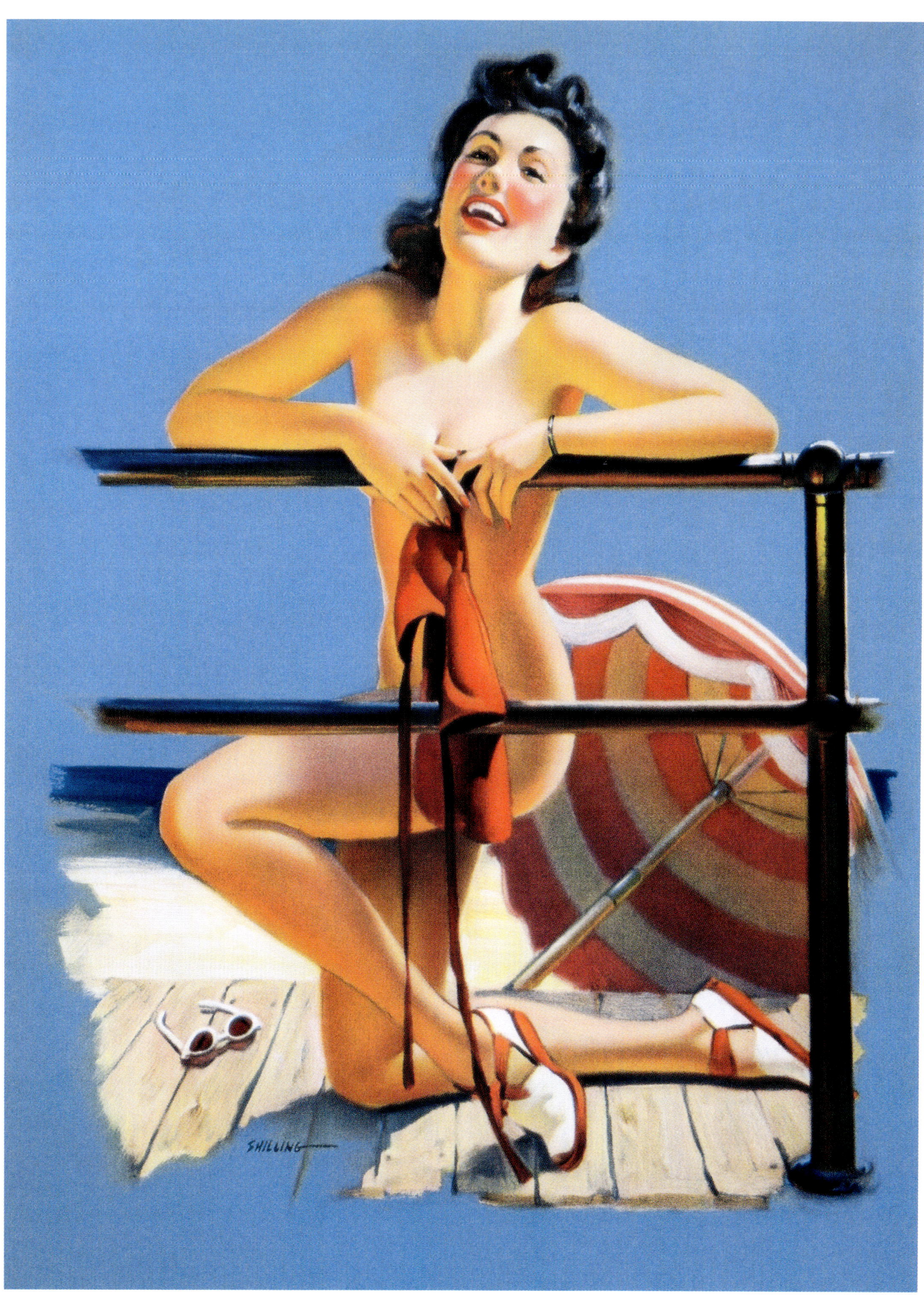
SHILLING